AF678540

The Long-Term Exit Strategy Blueprint

Build, Buy, and Sell Online Businesses That Create Lasting Wealth and Legacy

By Joe Correa

Published by Live Stronger Faster

Copyright © 2025 by Joe Correa

All rights reserved.

No part of this publication may be reproduced, distributed, or transmitted in any form or by any means—electronic, mechanical, photocopying, recording, or otherwise—without the prior written permission of the publisher, except in the case of brief quotations embodied in critical reviews and certain other noncommercial uses permitted by copyright law.

This book is for educational and informational purposes only. The author and publisher are not engaged in rendering legal, financial, or other professional advice. Readers should consult a qualified professional before making any financial decisions.

First Edition

Table of Contents

What if your exit strategy became your entry point to generational wealth?

Most people start businesses with one goal in mind: to make money now. They build fast, chase trends, and look for the next viral product or easy win. But rarely do they stop to ask: *How do I build something so valuable... someone else would pay handsomely to own it?*

This audiobook is not about shortcuts. It's about strategy. It's about playing the *long game.* You'll learn how to build online businesses with the specific intention of exiting — whether that means selling in 2 years for $100,000... or 10 years for $10 million.

Most importantly, you'll learn how to create digital businesses that don't just earn you money — they buy you **freedom**, protect your **legacy**, and allow you to **exit on your own terms.**

Why Most People Never Exit... and Why You Will

The truth is, **most online business owners never sell** — not because they don't want to, but because they don't know how.

Their books are a mess. Their business depends entirely on

them. They don't track KPIs, don't understand valuations, and haven't built transferable systems. When they finally do want to sell, no one wants to buy.

This audiobook will flip that script.

Whether you're just getting started or you've already launched your business, it's never too early (or too late) to start planning your exit. And the earlier you do it, the greater the leverage and value you'll build into every decision, hire, system, and sale.

Exits don't happen by accident. They happen by design. And you're going to learn exactly how to design yours.

What This Audiobook Will Teach You

Throughout this audiobook, you'll learn:

- The different types of digital businesses you can build or buy to later sell
- How to identify and create acquirable assets (what buyers actually pay for)
- How to increase the valuation of your business 2–5x with small changes

- How to make your business run without you (the most valuable asset of all)
- When to sell, how to price it, and how to negotiate the deal
- Where to list your business for sale or how to find strategic buyers
- And how to reinvest the profits into long-term wealth that serves your family for generations

Each chapter is packed with real-world examples, buyer psychology, proven systems, and a framework you can apply immediately — even if you're starting from scratch.

Why Exiting Matters (Even If You Never Sell)

Let's be clear: having a long-term exit strategy doesn't mean you have to sell.

In fact, some of the best digital business owners never exit because their businesses are so profitable and automated, they choose to keep them. But they still *built them to sell.* And that made all the difference.

A sellable business is:

- Clean, lean, and systematized

- Profitable and predictable
- Valuable with or without you involved
- Documented, delegated, and growing

Even if you never sell, you've now created a **cash-flowing asset**. And if life changes — if you need capital, want to pivot, or receive a strategic offer — you have the power to walk away with your biggest payday ever.

The Bigger Picture: Wealth and Legacy

For most of us, making money isn't the only goal. It's about freedom. Control over your time. The ability to travel, raise your kids, support your community, and sleep at night knowing that your family is secure.

Online businesses — when built correctly — offer that path.

But here's what very few people will tell you:

The real money is made on the exit.

Monthly income is great. But a strategic exit? That's the moment when years of work turn into a lump-sum life-changing event. It's the moment when a $5,000/month business gets sold for $200,000–$300,000. Or when a portfolio of cash-flowing websites creates a $1M+ sale – in a single transaction.

Whether you want to sell your business and retire early... flip a business every few years to stack capital... or hold for cash flow and exit only when the timing is right... this audiobook will give you the blueprint.

And unlike most business books, this one doesn't just stop at the sale.

We'll also explore what to *do* after the exit – how to reinvest, build passive wealth, and avoid the common mistakes entrepreneurs make after they sell.

The goal? Not just to build a business...

But to build a life.

One that creates freedom for you and opportunity for others – even after you're done working.

Ready to Begin?

So if you're ready to start thinking like a *founder* instead of a freelancer... If you want to create businesses that generate passive income *and* long-term wealth... If you want a proven roadmap to get from startup... to scale... to sold...

Then this audiobook will be your step-by-step guide.

Let's move on.

Chapter 1: Designing Your Business with the Exit in Mind

Why Starting with the End is the Smartest Move

Most entrepreneurs build businesses to earn income — not to exit. But the smartest entrepreneurs begin with the end in mind. They ask:

> "What would make someone want to buy this business 2, 5, or 10 years from now?"

This question changes everything. It impacts:

- How you structure operations
- What revenue models you choose
- What roles you delegate
- And how you track performance

Buyers don't just buy businesses — they buy income, systems, and freedom. The more predictable, transferable, and automated your business is, the higher your valuation.

The 4 Pillars of an Exit-Ready Business

To make your business attractive to buyers, build it around these four pillars:

1. Predictable & Profitable Revenue

- Recurring income (subscriptions, memberships) > one-off sales
- Diversified customer acquisition channels (not reliant on a single ad platform)
- Proven monetization with 12+ months of stable income

2. Owner Independence

- Can the business operate without you?
- Are there SOPs (Standard Operating Procedures)?
- Is your face or voice essential — or optional?

Use AI tools, freelancers, and automation to remove yourself from day-to-day operations.

3. Clean Financials

- Separate business and personal expenses

- Maintain profit & loss (P&L) statements, balance sheets, and bank records
- Use accounting software (e.g., QuickBooks, Wave, Xero) from day one

Buyers need to trust the numbers — and verify them fast.

4. Transferable Assets

- Are your systems, brand, and traffic transferable?
- Own your domain, email list, and trademarks
- Keep logins, contracts, and vendor agreements documented

Anything that can't be transferred hurts your valuation — or kills the deal.

Tools to Set Yourself Up for a Strong Exit

Use these early:

- **LLC or Corp**: Legal structure shows seriousness and allows clean acquisition
- **CRM**: Capture leads and track sales for proof of performance

- **SOP Templates**: Document tasks with Loom, Notion, or Google Docs
- **KPI Dashboards**: Track revenue, customer churn, conversion rates
- **Data Room Folder**: Keep everything ready to share with buyers (financials, traffic, contracts, growth plans)

The more prepared you are, the faster you can respond when the right buyer comes along — or when *you* decide it's time to sell.

Mindset Shift: You're Building an Asset, Not Just an Income Stream

An income stream pays your bills. An asset increases in value.

When you treat your online business like an asset, your decisions shift:

- You prioritize systems over hustle
- You delegate instead of doing everything
- You optimize for growth *and* sustainability

Start tracking your *Enterprise Value* — not just revenue. Ask: "If I stopped working tomorrow, what would someone pay for this business today?"

How to Stay Exit-Ready, Even While Scaling

- Revisit your valuation quarterly
- Keep updating your SOPs and team roles
- Stay lean and profitable — avoid overstaffing or bloated tools
- Build a "CEO Dashboard" to keep an eye on growth metrics

Whether you sell or not, you're building an asset that grows in value every month. That's how you create true financial leverage.

The kicker

Jacob was tired of the grind.

He'd built a digital product business that brought in $7,000 a month — decent income, decent freedom. But five years in, he was still answering support emails at midnight and fixing broken links himself. His business *was* his job.

Then came a wake-up call.

At a mastermind event, he met Claire — a woman who had sold her Shopify dropshipping brand for $380,000 just six months earlier. The kicker? Her business was making *less* than his.

“How?” Jacob asked.

She smiled. “Because I built it to run without me. My margins were clean, my numbers were documented, and the buyer saw potential without needing me around.”

That night, Jacob wrote one sentence on a blank sheet of paper: **“Build this to sell.”**

The next morning, he restructured everything.

He started by documenting every task he did daily — customer support, content uploads, email marketing. Using Loom, he recorded each task. Then he trained a VA in the Philippines to handle 80% of them.

He swapped his ad-hoc spreadsheets for real P&L statements using QuickBooks.

He stopped chasing new revenue streams and doubled down on recurring subscriptions that gave buyers predictability.

Within 12 months, his business hit $10K/month — with Jacob working just 5 hours a week.

Then, the call came.

A quiet email from a private equity buyer who had been browsing microacquisition platforms. “We love your brand,” it said. “Would you be open to discussing a purchase?”

Jacob felt a lump in his throat. He clicked over to his Google Drive folder — his SOPs, financials, and dashboards were already prepared.

He wasn’t just ready to sell. He’d *built* for this moment.

The deal closed 6 weeks later: $240,000 in cash, plus a 10% earn-out over the next 12 months.

Not bad for a guy who once thought he was just “making a living.”

As Jacob banked his wire transfer, one thought repeated in his mind:

> “I should’ve started with the exit in mind from day one.”

Now he teaches others how to build digital assets that free them — not trap them.

And it all began with that simple shift: **Think like an owner. Build like a seller.**

Chapter 2: Choosing the Right Business Model for Long-Term Exit Value

Why Your Business Model Dictates Your Exit Options

The type of business you build determines:

- Who will buy it
- How much they'll pay
- How long it will take to scale and exit

Some models are simple to grow but hard to sell. Others are slow to start but can command 6- or 7-figure exits if structured well.

So before you start or buy your next business, ask:

> "Is this the kind of business someone would *want* to buy?"

In this chapter, we'll compare top business models and highlight which ones offer the strongest combination of cash flow, scalability, and acquirability.

The Top 5 Exit-Friendly Online Business Models

1. Content Websites (Blogs, Niche Sites, Media Brands)

- Monetization: Ads, affiliate links, sponsorships, digital products
- Pros: Passive traffic, SEO value, low overhead
- Cons: SEO takes time; may depend on Google algorithm
- Exit Multiple: 30x–45x monthly profit

Best for: Long-term, semi-passive income with strong content libraries

2. Subscription Businesses (Memberships, SaaS, Online Courses)

- Monetization: Recurring monthly/annual subscriptions
- Pros: Predictable revenue, high lifetime value
- Cons: Requires churn management and customer success
- Exit Multiple: 40x–60x monthly profit

Best for: High-margin, scalable systems built on community or software

3. E-commerce (Shopify Stores, Amazon FBA, DTC Brands)

- Monetization: Physical product sales (with or without warehousing)
- Pros: Fast growth potential, large buyer pool
- Cons: Inventory risks, returns, supply chain issues
- Exit Multiple: 25x–45x monthly profit

Best for: Product developers and brand builders with strong logistics

4. Digital Products (Templates, Courses, Ebooks, Licenses)

- Monetization: One-time or recurring digital downloads
- Pros: High profit margins, low cost of delivery
- Cons: May be heavily dependent on the creator
- Exit Multiple: 30x–50x monthly profit (higher with automation)

Best for: Solopreneurs or educators creating evergreen content

5. Service Businesses with Productized Offers

- Monetization: Flat-fee packages, retainer clients

- Pros: Cash flow fast, scalable with VAs
- Cons: Lower exit multiple if client relationships aren't transferable
- Exit Multiple: 20x–35x monthly profit

Best for: Agencies that run lean or specialize in a niche

Factors That Increase Exit Value Regardless of Model

No matter which business model you choose, these *multipliers* boost your sale price:

1. **Recurring Revenue** – The more predictable your income, the more attractive your business.
2. **Diversified Traffic Sources** – Buyers love risk-spread businesses (not dependent on 1 platform).
3. **Team or SOPs in Place** – Makes your business transferable and low-maintenance.
4. **Customer Retention Metrics** – Strong lifetime value (LTV) and low churn signal a healthy business.
5. **Email List or Community** – Owned audiences are priceless.

Choosing Based on Your Strengths and Goals

Ask yourself:

- Are you a creator, operator, marketer, or investor?
- Do you want fast cash flow or long-term scale?
- Do you want to build, buy, or improve an existing business?

Example Paths:

- Creators → Content websites, digital products, courses
- Operators → Productized services, e-commerce
- Investors → Buy underperforming businesses, grow, then flip

Align your choice to your skills and your endgame.

The Hybrid Approach

Many successful digital entrepreneurs blend models. Example:

> Build a content site → capture email leads → sell a course or membership → upsell services

This multiplies your income *and* valuation — and appeals to a broader pool of buyers when it's time to sell.

Good bye 9-to-5

When Kendra started her online business, she didn't know what she wanted — just that she wanted *out* of her 9-to-5.

She launched a digital planner on Etsy, made a few hundred dollars, and thought she'd found her answer. But within three months, sales dipped. No traffic. No repeat customers. No system.

Feeling stuck, she stumbled on a podcast about *exit-ready* business models.

"What's your endgame?" the host asked. "If your business isn't sellable, it's not scalable."

Kendra paused. She had built a product… but *not* a business.

Determined to turn things around, she started researching. She realized that while one-time sales were nice, *recurring income* was what buyers really valued.

So she pivoted.

She created a $9/month digital membership where customers received exclusive new planners and templates each month. Then she rebuilt her email list with a freebie funnel and partnered with a few content creators for shout-outs.

In six months, she had 1,200 paying members.

No warehouse. No customer service headaches. Just simple digital delivery — and now, *predictable monthly income.*

Soon, Kendra systemized everything.

She used Zapier to automate new member emails. Canva templates were created once and reused monthly. A part-time VA handled questions.

Her profit margin soared past 85%. She worked less than 10 hours a week. And she had built a *real asset.*

One day, she received a message from a digital business broker.

"Would you consider selling? We have multiple buyers looking for digital memberships like yours."

Kendra wasn't even thinking about selling. But curiosity took over. She submitted her numbers.

A few weeks later, she got an offer: **$216,000** — all cash.

Kendra said yes.

She used the funds to invest in other digital assets — this time with exit value *as the starting point.*

She now owns a small portfolio of content websites and subscription products. Her mantra?

> "Always build with someone else's buyout in mind — even if you never sell."

Kendra's first business wasn't just a side hustle. It became her escape... and the launchpad for a long-term digital empire.

Chapter 3: Building Systems That Increase Business Value

Systems Are the Secret to Scale *and* Sale

When a buyer evaluates your business, they aren't just looking at how much you make — they want to know **how your business runs**.

> "If I take over tomorrow, will it collapse or continue running smoothly?"

That answer lies in your **systems**. Well-documented, repeatable systems make your business:

- More efficient
- Easier to delegate
- Far more valuable at exit

Without systems, your business is a job. With systems, it becomes a **machine**.

The 3 Core Types of Systems You Need

1. Operational Systems

These handle the daily work that keeps the business running.

Examples:

- Customer onboarding & support
- Order fulfillment (physical or digital)
- Content publishing schedule
- Invoicing and payment collection

Tools: Google Docs, Notion, Trello, ClickUp, Zapier

Tip: Use Loom to record your screen while doing tasks and turn those into SOPs.

2. Marketing Systems

Your ability to generate leads and sales without manual effort.

Examples:

- Email nurture sequences
- Paid ad funnels (Google, YouTube, Meta)
- SEO content calendar
- Affiliate or referral system

Tools: ActiveCampaign, ConvertKit, Meta Ads, Google Analytics

Tip: Set up automated campaigns that run even while you sleep. Predictable acquisition = higher valuation.

3. Reporting & Tracking Systems

Buyers want proof your business is stable and growing.

Examples:

- Weekly revenue reports
- Customer lifetime value (LTV) tracking
- Website traffic dashboards
- Conversion rate optimization logs

Tools: Google Data Studio, Baremetrics, ProfitWell, P&L spreadsheets

Tip: Build a CEO dashboard you review weekly. This also becomes part of your "data room" during due diligence.

How to Build SOPs (Standard Operating Procedures) That Actually Work

A good SOP answers:

- What to do
- When to do it

- How to do it
- Who does it

Structure:

1. **Title**: Clear and descriptive ("How to Publish a Weekly Blog Post")
2. **Purpose**: Why this SOP exists
3. **Tools Needed**: Software, logins, or assets
4. **Step-by-Step Instructions**: Screenshots, videos, checklists
5. **Owner**: Assigned team member

Tip: Store all SOPs in a single folder — a "Business Manual" you can hand off to a buyer.

Delegation Is a Value Multiplier

If you're doing everything yourself, your business can't scale — and most buyers will see it as a *liability*.

To fix this:

- Hire virtual assistants or part-time contractors
- Use AI for repetitive tasks (emails, video scripts,

editing, scheduling)

- Delegate decision-making to managers over time

Goal: The business should continue operating smoothly for at least 30 days without your input.

❖ How Systems Directly Impact Valuation

Businesses with strong systems:

- Sell faster
- Require less negotiation
- Receive higher multiples

Why? Because buyers can step in and **operate, grow, or flip the business** with confidence.

Think of systems as the **insurance policy** for your exit. They protect your income — and maximize your payday.

Systemize everything and anything

Nico was a solo founder with a profitable Shopify store.

He sold niche fitness gear — resistance bands, foam rollers, and weighted vests — and brought in about $20K/month. On the outside, it looked like a great business.

But inside? It was chaos.

Every order went through him. Every supplier email came to his inbox. When a customer needed a refund, Nico handled it personally. If Facebook Ads glitched, he scrambled at midnight.

When his mom got sick and he had to travel for two weeks, the entire business stalled. Orders piled up. Emails were missed. Revenue dropped 60%.

That's when he realized:

> *"I don't have a business — I have a fragile, high-paying job."*

After a hard conversation with a friend who had recently sold his e-commerce brand, Nico made a decision:

He was going to **systemize everything** — not just for sanity, but to make his business **sellable.**

He spent two weeks mapping every task he performed. Then, one by one, he:

- Recorded videos using Loom
- Wrote simple SOPs in Notion

- Hired a part-time VA from the Philippines to handle customer service
- Set up Zapier automations for tracking, fulfillment, and inventory updates
- Installed Google Data Studio to track his weekly KPIs in real time

Six months later, Nico's workweek was down to 5–8 hours.

Support tickets were answered in 12 hours or less — without him. Facebook Ads were running through an automated budget and audience testing system. His VA even managed returns and coordinated reorders with suppliers.

Most importantly: the business didn't collapse when he took a week off to visit family.

He'd built **systems, not stress**.

One day, a buyer on a marketplace emailed: "Your business looks clean. Can we see the SOPs and reports?"

Nico had it ready: a Google Drive folder with every task documented, a team org chart, and 12-month rolling revenue reports.

The buyer made an offer. Then another buyer outbid them.

In the end, Nico sold the business for $420,000.

As he walked away from the deal, Nico realized something deeper:

> "Systems weren't just for buyers. They were for *me* — to get my life back and build wealth on my own terms."

Now, every new business Nico starts begins with documentation from day one. He no longer builds jobs. He builds assets. And the secret was simple: **Systemize everything — early, often, and always.**

Chapter 4: Creating a Brand Buyers Fall in Love With

Why Brand Is Your Hidden Multiplier

When two businesses earn the same monthly profit, the one with a stronger **brand** almost always sells for more — often *30–100% more.*

> "People don't just buy numbers. They buy stories, trust, and potential."

A strong brand builds emotional connection, customer loyalty, and long-term equity that lives beyond the current owner. **Buyers see that — and pay for it.**

What Is a Brand, Really?

It's more than a logo or color scheme. A true brand is:

- **Identity** – Your mission, personality, tone of voice
- **Recognition** – Design, visuals, and consistency
- **Trust** – Proof of results, reviews, and social validation
- **Connection** – A community or audience that engages and buys again

In short: **Your brand is what people *say* about your business when you're not in the room.**

5 Elements That Make Your Brand Valuable to Buyers

1. Clear Positioning

Buyers want to know: Who is this for? What problem does it solve? What makes it different?

Tip: Use the "Only" Statement: "We are the **only** [type of business] that helps [specific audience] achieve [specific result] through [unique method]."

2. Consistent Visual Identity

A beautiful, consistent brand builds instant trust.

Must-haves:

- Logo, colors, typography, and design rules
- Website and sales pages that reflect your message
- Social media templates and post themes

Tip: Use Canva or hire a designer on Fiverr/Upwork to create a visual brand kit.

3. Customer Love (Social Proof)

Buyers want proof that customers trust you – and keep coming back.

Show:

- Video testimonials
- 5-star reviews
- Case studies or screenshots
- Social media engagement

Tip: Create a "Wall of Proof" folder — buyers love this during due diligence.

4. Content That Educates or Inspires

Educational or entertaining content builds brand equity over time.

Examples:

- Blogs and newsletters
- Short-form video (Reels, Shorts, TikToks)
- Long-form YouTube, podcast, or guides
- Lead magnets (ebooks, templates, quizzes)

Tip: Use content to build not just traffic — but *authority* in your niche.

5. Community or Audience Ownership

If you own the relationship (email list, followers, forum), you own the brand.

Buyers love:

- Active email list with high open/click rates
- Private Facebook Groups or Discord channels
- Loyal audience on IG, TikTok, or YouTube

Tip: Start building your list from day one. Email is still king.

How Branding Affects Valuation

Here's what strong branding does to your exit:

Business Type	**With Strong Brand**	**With Weak Brand**
Monthly Profit: $10,000	4x–6x Multiple	2x–3x Multiple
Valuation:	$480,000–$720,000	$240,000–$360,000

Same revenue. Different perception. Brand equity is real equity.

Avoid These Common Branding Mistakes

- No differentiation ("just another store/blog/course")
- Inconsistent messaging across platforms
- Overdependence on personal identity (harder to transfer)
- No content or community built around the brand

Instead, focus on **transferable identity** and **scalable personality**.

Build Your Brand as If You're Going to Sell It — Even If You Don't

A brand built for sale:

- Is recognizable without the founder
- Has clear customer avatars
- Can be carried forward by new leadership
- Is an asset — not just a marketing style

If someone else can grow your brand without changing the soul of it — you've built something great.

Building the Maya brand

Maya started her online wellness business with a single $19 ebook. No fancy logo. No paid ads. Just raw passion and Instagram.

She called it "SoulFuel Living" — a name that blended her love for fitness, mindfulness, and healthy living.

For the first year, she bootstrapped everything. She went from 1 sale a day... to 20... to launching a digital product bundle that pulled in $9,500 in a weekend.

But something strange happened.

People weren't just buying her content — they were **tagging her**, messaging her, and asking to be part of her "tribe." A community started forming.

That's when Maya made a decision:

> "This isn't just a product. This is a brand."

She hired a part-time designer to create a minimalist logo. She standardized her fonts and colors across her website and emails. She created a lead magnet: *"7 Days to SoulFuel Reset."*

In 3 months, her email list jumped to 10,000 subscribers. In 6 months, her brand was featured by two influencers she admired. In 12 months, she had a YouTube channel, two digital courses, and a $15/month membership.

More importantly, "SoulFuel Living" was now **known**.

People associated it with calm, energy, and transformation.

Then came the message.

A wellness company — backed by private investors — reached out to explore an acquisition. They had physical products and wanted to add a digital division.

They said: "We love your branding. Your audience *feels* like they belong."

Maya shared her media kit, brand assets folder, and her "wall of love" — a file packed with video testimonials, screenshots, and real stories from her customers.

The final offer?

$510,000 for her business, brand, and audience — plus a royalty agreement for any future course re-licensing.

She accepted.

But even more powerful than the money was the *validation*.

She had built something bigger than herself. A **brand** that someone else wanted to carry forward.

Now, Maya consults for early-stage creators, helping them build brands that buyers don't just respect — they *feel*.

And her advice is always the same:

> "Build your brand like someone's going to buy it.
>
> Because one day, someone probably will."

Chapter 5: Maximizing Monthly Profit While Staying Exit-Ready

Profit Is the Foundation of Valuation

Most online businesses are sold based on a **multiple of monthly or annual net profit**, not revenue.

> That means a $20,000/month revenue business earning $5,000 in net profit is often worth less than a $10,000/month revenue business earning $7,000 in net profit.

It's not what you make — it's what you keep. So if you want a valuable exit, your #1 job is to **increase profitability without compromising scalability or transferability.**

The Profit Formula Buyers Care About

Most buyers use a version of this simple formula:

Monthly Net Profit x Multiple = Valuation

Multiples usually range from **2.5x to 5x annual profit**, depending on:

- Model and niche
- Revenue consistency

- Owner involvement
- Brand strength
- Documentation and systems

Your goal: Boost profit *and* improve the factors that increase your multiple.

7 Ways to Increase Profit While Staying Exit-Ready

1. Raise Prices

Many entrepreneurs underprice themselves. Run A/B tests, reposition offers, and explore premium tiers.

Tip: Buyers love pricing power — it signals you aren't in a race to the bottom.

2. Cut Unnecessary Tools or Expenses

Audit tools, subscriptions, contractors, and platforms quarterly.

Tip: Keep your operating margin lean. Use free or bundled tools where possible (e.g., Canva Pro for team design + scheduling).

3. Productize Services or Offers

Create fixed-price packages that are easier to fulfill and easier to delegate.

Tip: The simpler the offer, the easier it is to systematize and scale.

4. Automate or Delegate Low-Value Tasks

Use automation (Zapier, AI, scheduling tools) and VAs to free up time and reduce payroll cost.

Tip: SOP every recurring task to make handoff seamless.

5. Increase Customer Lifetime Value (LTV)

Upsell existing customers. Add recurring revenue options. Offer bundled deals.

Tip: A $49/month plan over 12 months = $588/year per customer.

6. Reduce Refunds and Churn

Optimize onboarding, provide quick support, and set clearer expectations.

Tip: Buyers check refund and churn rates — stability wins over hype.

7. Improve Conversion Rates

Small changes in your funnel can mean thousands more per month.

Tip: Track each funnel stage, test headlines, improve copy, and remove friction.

Balance Profit Growth with Scalability

High profit is great — but not if it makes the business fragile.

Example:

- Firing your whole team might boost profit temporarily
- But buyers see it as unsustainable

Instead, optimize **efficient growth**:

- Scalable team structure
- Margin-friendly offers
- Repeatable systems

This makes your business profitable *and* attractive.

Monthly Profit Review Checklist

Every 30 days, ask:

- What's my true net profit this month?

- What recurring expenses can I eliminate or replace?
- What's my CAC (Customer Acquisition Cost) vs LTV?
- Is my profit growing or stagnating?

Tip: Keep a 12-month trailing P&L (Profit & Loss) file. Buyers will ask for it.

Make the business lean, clean, and profitable.

Andre was proud of his digital agency.

He offered funnel design for coaches and course creators. Business was booming — he made over $20,000 a month in revenue.

But when a potential buyer asked to see his books, reality hit: His net profit was less than $3,000/month.

Software expenses. Freelancers. Ads. Refunds. It all added up.

Worse? Without Andre, the business didn't run.

He realized:

> "I'm not building profit. I'm buying work."

Determined to turn things around, Andre made a bold move. He paused all new projects for 30 days. Instead, he focused on one goal: **Make the business lean, clean, and profitable.**

He started by auditing his tools. He canceled overlapping subscriptions, swapped expensive platforms for all-in-one tools, and cut $900/month instantly.

Then, he systemized his services.

He bundled his most-requested tasks into 3 clear packages. No more custom quotes. No more scope creep. Just scalable, repeatable products.

He trained two virtual assistants to handle 70% of delivery using Loom-recorded SOPs. His time in fulfillment dropped from 30 hours a week... to 6.

With time freed up, Andre optimized his sales funnel. He rewrote his offer page, added a one-click upsell, and created an evergreen email sequence.

In 60 days, his monthly revenue stayed the same... ...but profit tripled to $9,400/month.

The next time a buyer came calling, Andre was ready.

He showed them:

- Clean P&L statements
- Recurring revenue breakdown
- SOPs for every task
- A 90%+ customer satisfaction rate

The buyer loved it.

They offered $310,000 — all cash — for the business.

Andre took the deal. And in his final week as owner, he only worked 5 hours... and smiled the entire time.

His takeaway?

> "Don't just chase income. Design *profit* from the beginning.
>
> That's what buys your freedom."

Chapter 6: Preparing for Due Diligence and Buyer Negotiations

What Is Due Diligence — and Why It Makes or Breaks the Sale

Due diligence is the deep inspection phase where the buyer verifies everything you've claimed:

- Your traffic
- Your revenue
- Your systems
- Your intellectual property
- Your customer reviews and feedback
- Your liabilities and risks

> It's like a home inspection before closing — but for your business.

If you're not prepared, even a strong deal can collapse. But if you're ready, this is where you **gain trust, justify your price, and close the deal fast.**

Your Due Diligence Data Room: What to Prepare

Create a secure, shareable folder with everything a buyer might need. Include:

Financial Documents

- 12–24 months of P&L statements
- Tax returns (if applicable)
- Bank statements
- Breakdown of revenue by product/channel
- Invoices and receipts

Tip: Label everything clearly and organize by month or quarter.

Traffic & Analytics

- Google Analytics access (view-only)
- Social media insights
- Ad performance reports (Meta, Google, YouTube)
- Funnel stats (landing pages, conversion rates)

Tip: Include screenshots + shared dashboard links for fast review.

Operational Documents

- SOPs and workflows
- Org chart with responsibilities
- Tools and platforms list (with cost and usage)

Tip: Add a "transition plan" to show how the buyer can take over smoothly.

Legal & Ownership Docs

- LLC or corporation docs
- Domain registration & hosting info
- Trademarks, copyrights, licenses
- Vendor or affiliate agreements

Tip: Redact sensitive data until under NDA or letter of intent (LOI).

Customer & Brand Proof

- Reviews and testimonials
- Email list growth history and performance
- Churn/cancellation stats

- Support systems and satisfaction scores

Tip: A folder of real screenshots labeled "social proof" goes a long way.

How to Negotiate with Confidence

Most buyers will *not* accept your asking price right away. Be prepared for:

- Offer + earn-out (e.g., $100k upfront + $25k over 6 months)
- Revenue-share transitions (common in SaaS or content sites)
- Questions about risk, time involvement, or recent declines

Stay calm, data-driven, and outcome-focused.

Tip: Always know your "walk-away number" — and stick to it.

Common Red Flags That Scare Buyers (And How to Fix Them)

Red Flag	**How to Fix It**
Revenue dips	Explain seasonality with data + recovery strategy
Owner-dependent ops	Delegate and document before listing
Poor tracking or missing records	Get your books in order now
Legal/IP issues	Register trademarks, clean contracts
Unverified traffic sources	Use verified analytics platforms (e.g., GA4)

Sample Questions Buyers Might Ask You

1. How much time per week do you spend running this?
2. Who are your contractors or freelancers?
3. Why are you selling?
4. What are the biggest growth opportunities you haven't tapped yet?

5. What risks should I be aware of?

Tip: Answer openly but professionally. Transparency builds trust.

Final Advice: Make It Easy to Say Yes

- Be organized
- Be honest
- Be professional
- Have everything prepared *before* a buyer asks for it

The easier you make the process, the faster your payday.

The $310,000 valuation.

Carla had built her digital printables brand from her kitchen table. For 3 years, she uploaded planners, calendars, and meal templates to Etsy and her own Shopify store.

By year four, she was bringing in over $11,000/month — mostly passive income.

When she got a message from a digital business broker offering to list her business to their investor network, she thought, *"Why not? Let's see what it's worth."*

They suggested a $310,000 valuation.

She was stunned... and excited.

But then came due diligence.

The first buyer asked for P&L statements. Carla had rough spreadsheets. The second buyer wanted traffic analytics — she didn't have Google Analytics installed. Another asked about SOPs. She had none — just "everything in her head."

By the third buyer call, she was overwhelmed.

But instead of giving up, Carla got serious.

She spent two weeks building her "Data Room."

She downloaded and organized her Etsy sales reports. She installed GA4 and tracked Shopify traffic for 60 days. She hired a bookkeeper to build real P&L statements and retroactively reconcile the past 12 months. She created a Notion page with SOPs — from how to upload new products to how she handled customer inquiries.

She recorded short videos walking through each system.

Finally, she uploaded it all into a Google Drive folder titled: **"CarlaPrints Due Diligence – Confidential."**

She felt ready.

The next buyer — a content creator looking to acquire passive income brands — reviewed her folder and sent one email:

> "Impressive. When can we talk?"

Two weeks later, they made an offer: **$295,000 upfront, plus 5% of product royalties for 2 years.**

Carla accepted.

The buyer said, "You were organized, honest, and made this process effortless. That's rare — and why I moved so fast."

After the wire hit her account, Carla took a month off to travel.

On the flight home, she smiled — not just because of the money... ...but because she had turned a "one-woman shop" into a **saleable, desirable business.**

And all it took was preparing *like a pro.*

> "Buyers don't expect perfect," she now says. "They just want clarity and confidence. Give them both — and you'll always get offers."

Chapter 7: Structuring the Exit Deal to Maximize Your Payout

Not All Exits Are Created Equal

When it comes to selling your online business, **how the deal is structured** matters just as much as the price.

> Two offers can have the same headline number — but one puts cash in your pocket, and the other traps you in a risky earn-out.

This chapter is about how to **structure your deal strategically** so that you walk away with the most money, the least risk, and terms that protect your legacy.

The 5 Most Common Deal Structures

1. All-Cash Deal (Upfront Buyout)

- Buyer pays 100% of the agreed price at closing.
- Best for sellers who want a clean break.

Pros: Immediate payday, no risk of future performance.

Cons: Less common for larger deals, may lower the offer amount.

2. Cash + Earn-Out

- Buyer pays a portion upfront (e.g., 70%) and the rest based on performance milestones over time.

Pros: Potential for a higher total payout.

Cons: Risk if revenue drops or buyer mismanages the business.

3. Seller Financing

- Buyer pays a portion up front and the rest over time in fixed installments (like a loan).

Pros: Helps close deals faster, especially with newer buyers. Cons: If buyer defaults, you may have to reclaim the business or lose remaining payments.

4. Revenue Share

- Seller receives a percentage of revenue or profit for a defined period (e.g., 10% for 3 years).

Pros: Keeps you earning passively after exit.

Cons: Uncertain returns, no control post-sale.

5. Equity Roll-Over

- Seller keeps a percentage of ownership in the company after the sale.

Pros: Participate in future upside or exit if buyer grows the business.

Cons: Less liquidity, longer horizon.

Choosing the Right Deal Structure for *You*

Consider:

- How fast you want the money
- Whether you want to stay involved at all
- Your risk tolerance
- The buyer's track record

Your goal is not just to sell — it's to sell smart.

Key Terms You Must Understand (and Negotiate)

- **Letter of Intent (LOI):** Non-binding document that outlines the deal terms before due diligence.
- **Holdback:** A percentage of the price held in escrow to cover post-sale issues.
- **Non-Compete Clause:** Prevents you from launching a competing business for a period.

- **Transition Period:** Time during which you help the new owner take over (usually 30–90 days).
- **Asset vs. Stock Sale:** Asset sales are more common for small online businesses and protect the buyer from liability.

Tip: Hire a lawyer with M&A experience to review your contract. It's worth every dollar.

How to Push the Deal Value Higher (Even Without Raising Price)

- Add bonuses: email list, future product rights, affiliate deals
- License existing content for long-term reuse
- Include training or consultation hours post-sale
- Create marketing roadmaps or growth playbooks

These don't cost you much — but feel valuable to buyers.

Example: Two $300,000 Deals, Very Different Outcomes

Deal A	**Deal B**
$300k all cash	$150k cash + $150k earn-out
No transition required	6 months of support
Closed in 3 weeks	Closed in 3 months
Total: $300k guaranteed	Total: $150k guaranteed + risk

Always weigh *certainty vs. potential* — and protect your time, energy, and legacy.

Getting over exhaustion

Luis had done what many dream of.

He built a low-maintenance digital course business that taught freelancers how to build six-figure Upwork profiles. With just one VA and automated email funnels, he was clearing $12,000/month — with 90% margins.

After 3 years, he was ready to sell.

He listed the business for $360,000 on a curated marketplace. Within 2 weeks, he had 4 buyers interested.

One offer stood out:

> "$360,000 — but 50% upfront, 50% over 12 months based on performance."

Luis was tempted. But he had one problem: he was *done*. Mentally, emotionally, energetically.

He didn't want to stick around for a year just to *maybe* get the other half.

He asked the buyer: "What if we restructure the deal to $320,000 all cash instead?"

The buyer hesitated — then agreed.

It was $40,000 less on paper... But 100% guaranteed, with no strings attached.

Luis accepted.

Two days before the wire hit, another buyer emailed with a new offer:

> "$400,000 with a 2-year earn-out."

Luis didn't flinch.

He'd already learned the lesson:

> *The real value is not the biggest number. It's the freedom you walk away with.*

The deal closed fast.

Luis included:

- His SOPs
- 3 bonus courses he never released publicly
- A pre-recorded "training vault" for the new owner

The buyer was thrilled. The transition took less than 30 days.

Luis walked away with $320,000 in the bank — and peace of mind.

Later, when someone asked why he didn't hold out for more, he replied:

> "I didn't sell for the money. I sold for the *moment*.
>
> And that moment paid me everything I needed — all at once."

Now, Luis mentors other creators on deal structuring. And he always says the same thing:

> "Don't just close a deal.

Design it — to protect your future, your freedom, and your *final payout*."

Chapter 8: Reinvesting Your Exit Into Passive Wealth and Future Ventures

The Exit Is Just the Beginning

Congratulations — you sold your business.

Now what?

> The smartest entrepreneurs don't just sell for a payday — they use that payday to create **long-term freedom**.

This chapter is all about how to **reinvest your exit profits wisely** so that the money you made *keeps working for you* long after the deal closes.

Step 1: Build a Foundation of Financial Security

Before you reinvest a single dollar, protect your baseline.

Use a portion of your exit funds to:

- Pay off high-interest debt (especially credit cards or LOCs)
- Build or replenish your emergency fund (6–12 months expenses)

- Ensure adequate insurance (health, disability, liability)
- Set up basic estate planning and asset protection (LLCs, trusts)

Tip: Protecting your wealth is just as important as growing it.

Step 2: Reinvest in Income-Producing Assets

Once your financial foundation is secure, focus on **cash flow**.

Top reinvestment options post-exit:

1. Dividend-Paying Index Funds or ETFs

- Low maintenance, stable long-term growth
- Consider VTI, SCHD, or QQQM
- Target 3–10% annual returns depending on market cycles

2. Real Estate

- Buy-and-hold rental properties (residential or short-term)
- REITs (Real Estate Investment Trusts) for passive exposure

- Land or development parcels with growth potential

Tip: Use part of your exit cash as a down payment — leverage smartly with good terms.

3. Acquiring Smaller Online Businesses

- Buy underperforming content sites, SaaS tools, or digital products
- Fix and flip — or hold for recurring income
- Use platforms like Acquire.com, Flippa, or Empire Flippers

4. Angel Investing or Syndicates

- Higher risk, higher reward
- Invest in startups in industries you know
- Look for asymmetric bets with strong teams

Tip: Don't invest more than 10–15% of your portfolio in high-risk deals.

Step 3: Start or Scale Your Next Venture (Optional)

You don't have to build again — but many do.

If you do:

- Start smaller, smarter, and more automated
- Focus on exit-friendly models from the start
- Use your credibility and capital to launch faster

Tip: Consider partnerships, licensing, or joint ventures instead of starting from scratch.

Step 4: Create a System for Wealth Growth

Now that you have money, you need a **system** to manage it.

- Use a financial advisor or CPA who understands digital businesses
- Set monthly or quarterly wealth reviews
- Separate your investment accounts from daily spending
- Track your Net Worth and Cash Flow like a business

Tip: Treat your personal wealth like your most important company.

Avoid These Post-Exit Mistakes

- **Lifestyle creep** (spending dramatically more without ROI)
- **Overconfidence** in new risky projects
- **No plan** (burning through cash with no structure)
- **Tax surprises** (not setting aside enough for capital gains)

Always remember:

> *Freedom isn't in the sale. It's in how you use the money after the sale.*

Final Thought: Don't Just Exit a Business. Enter a New Life.

The goal was never just the check. It was what the check made possible.

Use this moment to:

- Invest in time freedom
- Build legacy wealth
- Say no to burnout and yes to optionality
- Help others or give back with intention

You didn't just sell a business. You **bought a future** — now make it count.

How Olivia decided to build with it.

Olivia sat quietly as the wire transfer hit her bank account: **$480,000.**

Her Shopify store — a niche apparel brand she'd started in college — was now in someone else's hands.

No more order tracking. No more supplier calls at 3 a.m. No more weekends buried in spreadsheets.

Just one big question remained:

> "What now?"

The old Olivia would've celebrated by upgrading her car and planning a month in Europe. But she'd been through too much — the long nights, the debt, the stress.

She didn't want to burn the money. She wanted to **build with it.**

So she sat down with a notebook and wrote three words: **Protect. Grow. Give.**

First, she paid off her lingering student loan and credit card debt – gone.

Then, she opened a high-yield savings account with 12 months of personal runway. She created a simple LLC to manage her investments and protect her assets.

Then came phase two.

She split the remaining money into three buckets:

- **50%** went into dividend-paying ETFs and blue-chip stocks.
- **25%** went toward a down payment on a duplex rental property near her hometown.
- **25%** was her "opportunity fund" – money to invest in digital assets or new ideas.

Within six months, the duplex was rented out. Her ETF portfolio was growing steadily. And she used part of her "opportunity fund" to acquire a small digital download shop from a stay-at-home mom for just $8,000 – it generated $400/month with zero ads.

Olivia wasn't working 60-hour weeks anymore. She checked her metrics monthly. She read, traveled, and mentored other first-time founders online.

One night, she had dinner with an old friend who asked, "Don't you miss the hustle?"

She smiled and said:

> "I don't miss chasing money. I like watching it grow without me now."

Olivia had exited one chapter — and entered another.

Her legacy wasn't the store she sold. It was the **life she designed after it.**

Chapter 9: Avoiding Regret, Post-Sale Pitfalls and How to Transition Smoothly

Selling Feels Like Winning... Until It Doesn't

While a business exit should be exciting, many founders experience a wave of unexpected feelings after the sale:

- Emptiness or loss of purpose
- Seller's remorse or "Did I sell too early?"
- Anxiety over money management
- Identity crisis after years of hustle

That's because you're not just selling a business – you're closing a personal chapter.

This chapter will help you **avoid post-sale regret**, transition smoothly, and create clarity for your next season.

❖ 7 Common Post-Exit Mistakes (And How to Avoid Them)

1. Spending Too Fast

The rush of a wire transfer can trigger lifestyle creep: new cars, big trips, lavish upgrades.

Avoid: Let your cash sit for 30–60 days before making any major decisions. Emotion fades, clarity grows.

2. Jumping Into Another Business Too Quickly

Many sellers feel lost without a project — and leap into a new venture without rest or purpose.

Avoid: Take a pause. Reflect on what you want next. Your *next* business should be a conscious choice, not a reaction.

3. Failing to Prepare for Emotional Impact

Even a good exit can feel like loss. Especially if your identity was tied to the business.

Avoid: Have a plan for your time, creativity, and purpose post-sale. Journal. Travel. Coach. Mentor. Reconnect with life outside business.

4. Ignoring the Transition Plan

If you promised 30–90 days of support post-sale, don't wing it.

Avoid: Create a structured onboarding guide for the buyer. Set boundaries and deliverables. Protect your time.

5. Overcommitting to the Buyer

Some buyers may try to squeeze "extra" out of your support period.

Avoid: Set clear terms in your LOI and contract. Track hours if necessary. Be helpful — not handcuffed.

6. Failing to Reinvest Strategically

Many sellers park their money and let inflation erode its power.

Avoid: Create an investment strategy within 90 days. Think long-term cash flow and capital preservation.

7. Losing Focus on Health, Relationships, and Purpose

Burnout doesn't magically disappear after a sale. Take time to heal.

Avoid: Neglecting wellness, family, and self-development. Wealth without health is just stress in disguise.

Your Post-Exit Transition Checklist

1. **Conduct a Closing Debrief:** Reflect on what worked, what didn't, and what you learned.

2. **Update Your Personal Financial Plan:** Meet with a CPA or advisor to adjust goals, taxes, and investments.

3. **Block 30–60 Days for Reset:** No business launches. Use the time to reconnect with yourself.

4. **Transfer Responsibilities Cleanly:** Use a "handover document" with passwords, SOPs, vendors, etc.

5. **Celebrate Intentionally:** You've done something 99% of people never do — honor it.

Design Your Next Season With Intention

Ask yourself:

- What do I want to create now that I don't *have* to work?
- What kind of work would feel meaningful — even if I don't need the money?
- What relationships, hobbies, or causes have I neglected?

You exited the business. Now, **enter the life** you actually want.

How Malik got over feeling lost.

Malik had always dreamed of a big exit. After four years of growing his YouTube automation agency, he finally sold it for **$620,000**.

The deal closed on a Friday. By Monday, Malik didn't know what to do with himself.

He refreshed his bank account three times a day... but felt nothing.

For months, he had imagined a celebratory trip to Dubai, a new Tesla, and total peace.

Instead, he was restless, irritable — even anxious.

His friends were congratulating him. His family said, "You've made it."

But Malik didn't *feel* like he made it. He felt **lost**.

He tried to start a new business immediately — a coaching program. It flopped.

He tried investing in startups — and lost $25,000 in a bad bet.

Nothing filled the void.

Then, after a quiet dinner with his sister, she asked:

"Did you ever stop to process what just happened?"

He hadn't.

So Malik slowed down.

He booked a two-week retreat in Costa Rica — no laptop, no plans. There, between hikes and quiet journaling, he made a new commitment:

> "I'm going to let this chapter end before I force the next one to begin."

He returned home and created a new routine:

- Morning meditation and walks
- Daily reading and reflection
- Weekly volunteer work with young entrepreneurs
- Monthly check-ins with his advisor to manage his money

He didn't start a new business for six months. And when he did, it was one that lit him up — a podcast and media brand for exited founders navigating *what comes next.*

The new Malik wasn't chasing the next 6-figure deal.

He was living with **clarity**, purpose, and energy. And ironically, that alignment made him more successful than ever.

When asked what advice he'd give first-time sellers, he says:

> "Don't just plan the deal. Plan the *after*.
>
> Because the real freedom isn't in the check.
>
> It's in who you become when you finally have nothing to prove."

Chapter 10: Your Legacy Exit — How to Sell for Impact, Not Just Income

Why Legacy Matters More Than Just the Payday

You didn't spend years building your business just for a wire transfer. You built it because you cared. You built it with heart, hustle, and purpose.

> A legacy exit isn't just about how much you earn — it's about **how your business lives on** after you're gone.

In this final chapter, you'll learn how to exit in a way that creates:

- Personal fulfillment
- Ongoing impact
- Positive ripple effects beyond profit

What Is a Legacy Exit?

A legacy exit is a business sale that:

- Aligns with your values
- Serves your audience long after you leave

- Benefits your family or community
- Honors the mission that started it all

This doesn't mean you settle for less. It means you **sell with purpose** — not just price.

5 Ways to Turn Your Exit Into a Legacy

1. Choose the Right Buyer

Don't just pick the highest offer. Pick the buyer who will:

- Protect the brand's mission
- Serve your customers with care
- Keep your team (if applicable)

Tip: Ask buyers about their 12-month and 5-year plans for your brand.

2. Negotiate Beyond the Dollar

Include legacy-minded terms:

- Maintain access to your product library or community
- Guarantee team retention for a period
- Request public credit as founder or advisor

Tip: Your name still holds value — protect how it's used.

3. Give Back from the Exit

Decide in advance if a portion of your exit will:

- Go to a charity or cause you care about
- Fund scholarships, nonprofits, or education
- Support your family or community in lasting ways

Tip: Set this up with your financial advisor or a donor-advised fund (DAF).

4. Document Your Journey

Turn your experience into something that lives on:

- Write a book, create a mini-course, or record your lessons
- Mentor new founders
- Share the real story — the wins *and* the wounds

Tip: Your story may help others more than you know.

5. Keep Ownership of Your Values

Even if you let go of the business, don't let go of the mission.

You can:

- Launch a new project with a similar message
- Start a foundation or initiative
- Continue speaking or creating under your personal brand

Tip: Values can't be sold — but they *can* be scaled.

Questions to Guide Your Legacy Exit

Ask yourself:

- Who will benefit most from my business once I leave?
- What impact do I want this brand to have after I'm gone?
- What would make this feel *complete*, not just profitable?

> Legacy isn't built in the exit contract — it's built in the intention behind it.

Final Reflection: The Business Is Temporary. The Impact Is Forever.

You built something meaningful. And now, you're choosing how that meaning continues.

Whether you reinvest in people, causes, communities, or your next idea — **do it with heart**.

The best exits don't just pay well. They **live well** — in the people they touched and the values they preserved.

You've earned this moment. Now lead it well.

Sarah's automated content at scale.

Sarah had built her business on a simple promise: Help moms find balance between health and home.

Her online membership, "Mindful Mom Daily," served over 3,000 members — offering meal plans, fitness challenges, mindset coaching, and live Q&As.

After 6 years, she felt the tug: It was time to move on.

But every time an offer came in, she hesitated.

> "What if they ruin what I built? What if they turn this into just another sales funnel?"

She finally received a $750,000 offer from a venture-backed wellness brand. But the buyer made it clear — they'd rebrand the entire thing.

"No community. No coaching. Just automated content at scale."

Sarah declined — even though it was her biggest offer yet.

She told her husband that night:

> "I'm not just selling a business. I'm handing off a *mission*. And I need it to go to someone who gets that."

Three weeks later, she received a message from a woman named Jordan.

Jordan had built a postpartum care brand and wanted to expand into lifestyle and digital education.

She had followed Sarah for years. She said:

> "You created something that changed my life after my second baby. I'd be honored to keep it going."

They talked for hours.

Sarah showed her systems, the member stories, the community messages.

Jordan cried.

The offer was smaller: $600,000.

But it came with a promise:

- The community would stay
- The brand would remain "Mindful Mom Daily"
- Sarah would be listed as "Founder Emerita" on the About page

Sarah accepted.

And it was the happiest she'd felt in months.

After the deal closed, Sarah used part of the funds to:

- Start a nonprofit for single moms
- Build a scholarship fund for mental health coaches
- Take a long overdue road trip with her family

She never regretted taking the lower offer.

> "Because the mission lived on," she says. "And the business kept changing lives — with or without me."

That's a **legacy exit**.

Epilogue: This Is Just the Beginning

You've made it to the end of this audiobook – but if you're doing this right, it's only the **beginning** of something far greater.

You now have the complete roadmap to not only build and sell an online business – but to do it with *intention*, *strategy*, and *heart*. Whether you're starting from scratch, scaling what you've already built, or preparing to exit something valuable, the tools are now in your hands.

But the real question is:

What kind of empire will you build with them?

Because the entrepreneurs who make the biggest impact – and the biggest profits – are those who:

- Design with the end in mind
- Focus on assets, not just income
- Automate without losing soul
- Grow teams, not just traffic
- And exit not just for dollars... but for **meaning**

Maybe this audiobook planted your first seed. Maybe it confirmed what you already suspected: You don't need permission to build something great — just a blueprint and the courage to follow it.

The online world is overflowing with opportunity. You've already proven you're different — by listening, learning, and *finishing* this guide.

Now it's time to take the next step.

Build boldly. Sell smart. And leave behind something that matters.

Because in the end, it's not just about what you *exit from* — it's about what you're stepping *into*.

www.ingramcontent.com/pod-product-compliance
Lightning Source LLC
LaVergne TN
LVHW022017200926
848481LV00007B/2438